Dec 2016

BRITANNICA BEGINNER BIOS

SITTING BULL

LAKOTA TRIBAL CHIEF AND LEADER OF NATIVE AMERICAN RESISTANCE

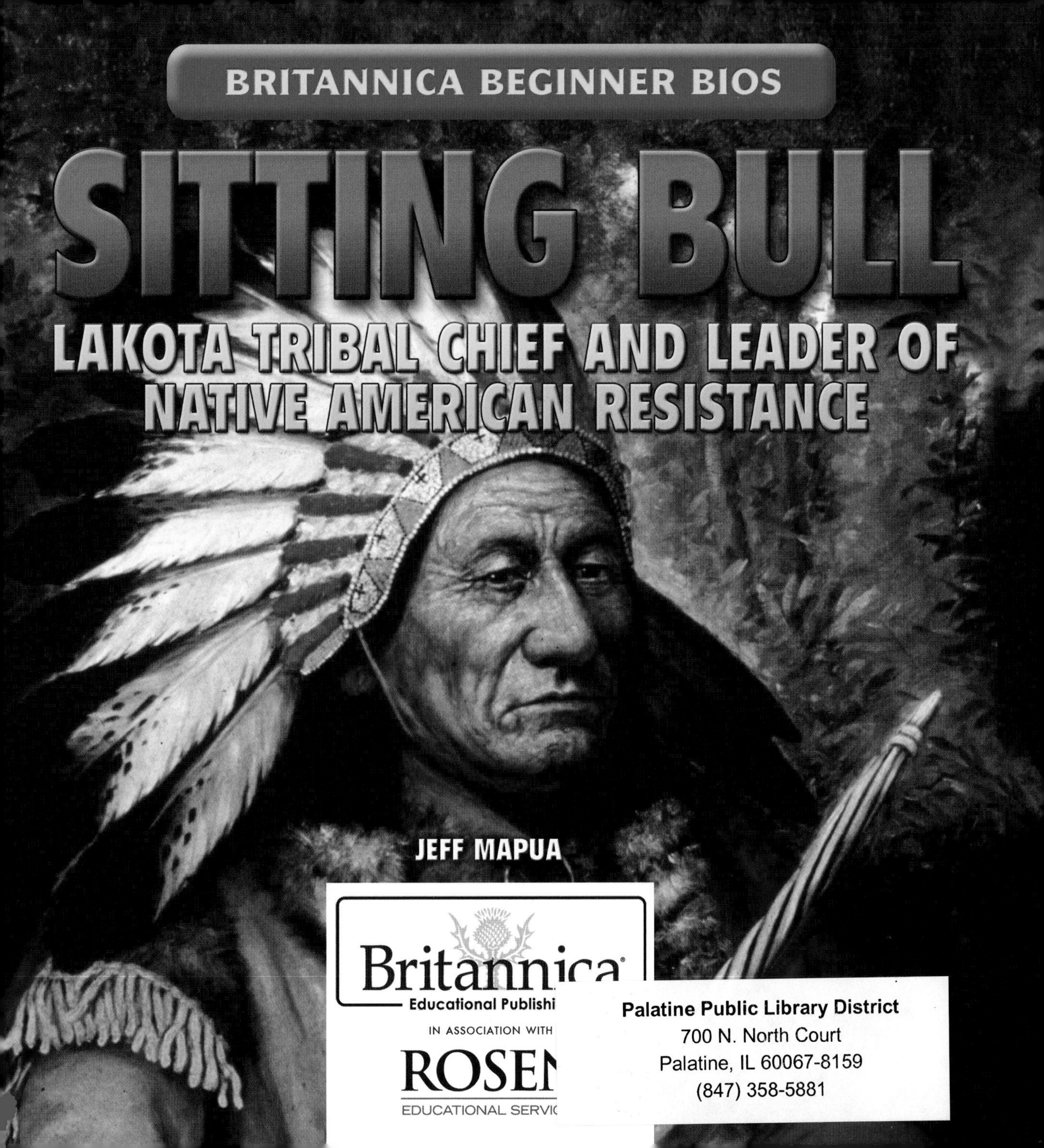

JEFF MAPUA

Britannica
Educational Publishi

IN ASSOCIATION WITH

ROSE
EDUCATIONAL SERVIC

Published in 2016 by Britannica Educational Publishing (a trademark of Encyclopædia Britannica, Inc.) in association with The Rosen Publishing Group, Inc.
29 East 21st Street, New York, NY 10010

Distributed exclusively by Rosen Publishing.
To see additional Britannica Educational Publishing titles, go to rosenpublishing.com.

First Edition

Britannica Educational Publishing
J.E. Luebering: Director, Core Reference Group
Mary Rose McCudden: Editor, Britannica Student Encyclopedia

Rosen Publishing
Jacob R. Steinberg: Editor
Nelson Sá: Art Director
Nicole Russo: Designer
Cindy Reiman: Photography Manager
Karen Huang: Photo Researcher

Cataloging-in-Publication Data

Mapua, Jeff.
 Sitting Bull : Lakota tribal chief and leader of Native American resistance/Jeff Mapua.—First edition.
    pages cm—(Britannica beginner bios)
 Includes bibliographical references and index.
 ISBN 978-1-68048-257-7 (library bound) — ISBN 978-1-5081-0062-1 (pbk.) — ISBN 978-1-68048-315-4 (6-pack)
 1. Sitting Bull, 1831-1890—Juvenile literature. 2. Dakota Indians—Biography—Juvenile literature. 3. Hunkpapa Indians—Biography—Juvenile literature. 4. Little Bighorn, Battle of the, Mont., 1876—Juvenile literature. I. Title.
 E99.D1.M27 2016
 978.0049752440092—dc23
 [B]

2015014102

Manufactured in the United States of America.

CONTENTS

CHAPTER ONE

MORE THAN A LEGEND

In late June 1876, soldiers of the U.S. Cavalry, a group of troops on horse-back, fought a major battle against a group of Native American warriors from several different **TRIBES.** One of the leaders of the Native Americans was a powerful man known as Sitting Bull.

Sitting Bull was an important Native American leader. He fought for his people all his life.

This 1857 illustration shows a group of Native Americans attacking white settlers who were moving west.

The relationship between the Native Americans and the U.S. government had been tense for many years. Settlers moving to the West had come into conflict with Native Americans who lived there. The U.S. government wanted to protect the settlers. Troops tried to force the Native Americans to move to reservations. Sitting Bull and others fought back, most notably at the Battle of the Little Bighorn.

The Battle of the Little Bighorn

In June 1876, U.S. soldiers were looking for a large group of Native Americans led by Sitting Bull. Hundreds of soldiers approached the valley where they heard the group may have camped. However, they

The Battle of the Little Bighorn was a major victory for the Native American tribes.

> ## Quick Fact
>
> **The Battle of the Little Bighorn is named after the Little Bighorn River, near where the battle was fought. It is also called Custer's Last Stand, after the leader of the U.S. troops.**

were spotted. Lieutenant Colonel George Armstrong Custer, the leader of the U.S. soldiers, ordered his troops to attack. To their surprise, more than a thousand Native American warriors were waiting for them.

Sitting Bull's warriors used their hunting skills in battle. In the end, the Native American tribes won. Sitting Bull would forever be remembered for defeating Custer and his troops.

But who was Custer, and why was he fighting the tribes? Where were the reservations that the U.S. government set up for the Native Americans? Who was Sitting Bull? The answers to these questions reveal an important part of the history of the United States.

CHAPTER TWO

EARLY LIFE

Many people know the name Sitting Bull. They may know that he was involved in a famous battle. But Sitting Bull was not always famous. Before he led his people in the Battle of the Little Bighorn, Sitting Bull had to prove himself as a warrior and chief first.

The Lakota People

Sitting Bull was a member of the Teton Sioux. The Sioux are a group of Native Americans who speak similar languages. The Teton are one of the three main groups of Sioux, based on the languages they traditionally spoke. The Teton spoke Lakota. The Santee spoke Dakota, and the Yankton spoke Nakota. The groups are

Sitting Bull was a Sioux Indian. The Sioux people have a very rich culture and history.

often known by the name of their language, so the Teton are called the Lakota.

The Sioux originally lived near Lake Superior in what is now Minnesota. In the mid-1700s, wars with other Native American tribes made the Sioux move west. The Lakota went the farthest west. They moved to the Black Hills region of the Dakota Territory. (This region is now part of western South Dakota and eastern Wyoming and Montana.) Sitting Bull was born in about 1831 near the Grand River in what is now South Dakota.

Jumping Badger

When he was born, Sitting Bull's parents gave him the name Jumping Badger. It was the first of many names in his life.

As a child, Jumping Badger was cautious. He always thought before acting. Many others did not see him as careful though. Some people thought he was **FEEBLE**. They gave him the nickname Hunkesni, which means "slow."

Vocabulary Box

Someone who is **FEEBLE** does not have strength or endurance.

A Young Warrior

Jumping Badger's uncle, Four Horns, was a leader of the Lakota people. He taught his nephew how to hunt and to ride a horse.

When he was fourteen years old, Jumping Badger fought in his first battle. Hunkesni, the so-called

This drawing by his uncle shows Sitting Bull's first victory in battle, at the age of fourteen.

Quick Fact

When young Lakota accomplish something important, they are given new names to honor them. Jumping Badger received his father's name, Sitting Bull, after his first battle at age fourteen.

"slow" child, impressed everybody with his battle skills. The young man helped carry out an impressive raid on an enemy group of Native Americans. To honor him, Jumping Badger's father passed on his own Sioux name, Tatanka Iyotake, which means Sitting Bull. His father, in turn, took the name Jumping Bull. With his new name, Sitting Bull's bravery and courage became well known among his people.

Sitting Bull continued to win battles against other Native American tribes. He also became part of two warrior societies. They were called the Strong Heart and Kit Fox societies. He showed himself to be a strong fighter. The Lakota also believed Sitting Bull was a Wichasha Wakan, or holy man.

Family Life

A Lakota man could have many wives as long as he could provide food and shelter for them. Sitting Bull had fives wives during his lifetime.

Sitting Bull also had many children. In addition to the children he had with his wives,

Sitting Bull had several children and adopted more. Some of his family is shown here.

Sitting Bull took in other children. He adopted a boy from another tribe and mentored his nephew.

CHAPTER THREE

THE BUILDUP TO BATTLE

Sitting Bull's life was not easy. As a warrior, he had to defend his home against other Native American tribes. He also had to defend his home against a new threat: white settlers.

Vocabulary Box

People who are NOMADIC do not have a permanent home. They wander from place to place, setting up temporary homes as they move.

Protecting Their Land

Sitting Bull belonged to a specific tribe of Lakota Indians called the Hunkpapa. The Hunkpapa were **NOMADIC** and warlike. They followed bison across the plains. They ate bison meat and used bison skins to make tepees and clothes. By the middle 1800s white settlers were invading Sioux hunting grounds. This made it hard for Sioux to get food. The U.S. government wanted to separate the Indians from the settlers by moving the Indians to reservations. Each tribe was assigned its own area. The Sioux reservation was in the Dakotas and parts of Nebraska, Montana, and Wyoming.

Nomadic tribes often lived in tepees, which made it easier to move.

The Hunkpapa were ready to fight to protect the Sioux land. Sitting Bull's first battle with white soldiers happened in June 1863. For the next five

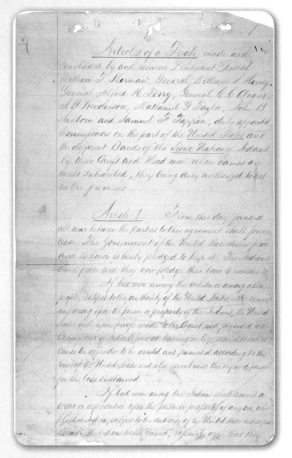

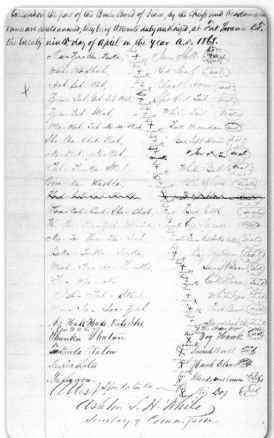

The Sioux and the U.S. government signed the Treaty of Fort Laramie in 1868.

years, he often led battles against the U.S. Army and white settlers to protect his people's land. Sitting Bull was named chief of the entire Sioux nation in about 1867.

In 1868, some of the Sioux and the U.S. government agreed to stop fighting. Certain Sioux leaders signed a peace agreement called the Treaty of Fort Laramie. This treaty promised the Sioux people their own reservation for only their use if they gave up land to the government.

Quick Fact

In the mid-1870s, gold was discovered in the Black Hills region of the Dakota Territory. White settlers moved in looking for gold. The arrival of miners upset Native Americans and stirred them for battle.

White settlers searching for gold disrupted the lives of Native Americans in the area.

Moving to a reservation meant the Sioux would give up their nomadic lifestyle. Some Lakota leaders, including Sitting Bull and Crazy Horse, did not want to move to a reservation. They were still ready to fight.

Lieutenant Colonel George Armstrong Custer

In late 1875, the government ordered the remaining Native Americans to leave their land. Sitting Bull and his people refused to go. The U.S. Army was sent to remove them.

One of the U.S. Army commanders was George Armstrong Custer. During the American Civil War, Custer had fought for the North. He was famous for being very brave and aggressive. When the Civil

War ended, Custer became lieutenant colonel of an army unit called the 7th Cavalry.

In 1876, Sitting Bull gathered his own people along with some members of the Cheyenne and Arapaho tribes. He told them he had a vision that soldiers would fall on their camps like grasshoppers from the sky.

On June 25, 1876, Sitting Bull's vision came true. Custer and his soldiers rode into the valley of the Little Bighorn River to attack the Native Americans. Custer's attack was one of the greatest disasters in the history of the U.S. Army.

The graves of General Custer and other soldiers stand at the site of the Battle of the Little Bighorn.

CHAPTER FOUR

AFTER THE BATTLE

The Battle of the Little Bighorn was a short-lived victory for the Native Americans. When the battle ended, Custer and all of his soldiers were dead. However, the war was far from over for the surviving tribes.

A Native American artist painted the Battle of the Little Bighorn on this buffalo hide in 1878.

The Fight Goes On

After the Battle of the Little Bighorn, the U.S. government became more determined to fight the Native Americans. The U.S. Army sent more troops to fight the Sioux and other tribes. The Sioux continued to fight against the U.S. troops. Sitting Bull won many more battles, but his people were in trouble.

As in the past, the Sioux hunted bison for food. As more settlers moved onto the Great Plains, the bison began to die out. In 1877, Sitting Bull led his people to Canada to look for food and to escape the U.S. Army. They stayed in Canada for four years. However, in 1881, a lack of food forced him and his people to **SURRENDER**. The Native Americans lost their land and got nothing in return.

Vocabulary Box

To **SURRENDER** means to give over to somebody else's power or control, especially by that person's force.

21

Sitting Bull settled on a reservation but remained outspoken. He complained when the government sold tribal lands to white settlers.

Buffalo Bill's Wild West Show

The U.S. government wanted to keep Sitting Bull quiet. In 1885, they allowed him to join Buffalo Bill's Wild West show. The show was run by a man named William Frederick Cody, better known as Buffalo Bill. The show featured entertainment such as shooting and buffalo (bison) hunts.

The show helped Sitting Bull gain international fame. He earned $50 a week to ride once around the arena at each show. He also earned money by signing autographs and taking pictures with

The Sioux had to move onto reservations such as this one in South Dakota.

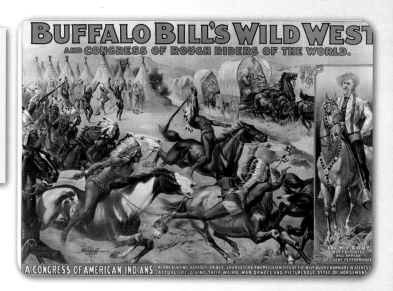

Buffalo Bill brought the Wild West to paying audiences around the country.

fans. Sitting Bull toured for only four months. During this time he shook hands with President Grover Cleveland. Sitting Bull felt that he was still respected.

Fighting Until the End

In 1889, a Native American religious movement called the Ghost Dance became popular. The movement promised that the white settlers would disappear from Native American lands and that the traditional way of life would return. Afraid that Sitting Bull would cause trouble, Native American police took action.

23

A memorial stands over Sitting Bull's grave in Mobridge, South Dakota.

On December 15, 1890, Native American police arrested Sitting Bull. His followers objected and tried to stop the arrest. Sitting Bull was killed in the fighting. Sitting Bull was buried at Fort Yates in North Dakota. In 1953, his remains were moved to his people's land in Mobridge, South Dakota.

SITTING BULL'S LEGACY

Sitting Bull has remained an important figure in American history. He was respected by the Native Americans for his courage and wisdom. He was feared by settlers and the U.S. Army for his **DETERMINATION** to protect his tribe's land.

Vocabulary Box

When somebody has DETERMINATION, he or she is very clear and firm about his or her beliefs.

Sitting Bull is remembered by Native Americans as a hero and a leader.

Sitting Bull helped unite the Sioux tribes in their struggle against white settlers. Sitting Bull became a symbol to all Native Americans. He represented a way of life that many Native American people lost. He fought to keep his culture and traditions alive until the day he died. Sitting Bull was a spiritual, political, social, and economic leader.

Quick Fact

In 1996, an important Sioux college in Fort Yates, North Dakota, was renamed Sitting Bull College in honor of the tribal chief's legacy.

The Battle of the Little Bighorn is also a powerful symbol today. People from around the world visit the location of the battle. It is a reminder of the important Native American culture that was destroyed by white settlement.

Renaming the Monument

After the Battle of the Little Bighorn, people fought over the battlefield itself. For many years it was a monument to Lieutenant Colonel Custer and his soldiers. It was a national cemetery. It became known as the Custer Battlefield.

The memorials at Little Bighorn Battlefield honor both Native Americans and U.S soldiers who died in the battle.

Over time, people fought to honor the Native Americans who fought in the battle as well. People wanted to honor the role Sitting Bull played in protecting his people. They wanted the battlefield to have a neutral name. On December 10, 1991, the name was changed to Little Bighorn Battlefield. Memorials for the Native Americans who fought were added. Sitting Bull would be proud to know his people were finally honored on their own land.

TIMELINE

About 1831: Sitting Bull is born. His parents name him Jumping Badger.

1845: Jumping Badger is honored by his tribe after his first raid. He is given the new name Tatanka Iyotanka, which means Sitting Bull.

1846: Sitting Bull receives his first red feather for a war injury.

1851: Sitting Bull marries his first wife, Light Hair.

1859: Sitting Bull's father dies in battle.

1861: Sitting Bull marries his second wife, Snow-on-Her.

1867: Sitting Bull becomes the head chief of the Sioux tribes.

1868: Certain Sioux leaders sign the Fort Laramie Treaty. These Sioux leaders agree to move to reservations. Sitting Bull and other leaders are against the treaty.

1871: Sitting Bull marries his third wife, Scarlet Woman.

1872: Sitting Bull marries his final wives, Seen-by-her-Nation and Four Robes.

1874: Gold is discovered in the Black Hills located on the Great Sioux Reservation.

1875: The Sioux resisting white settlement are ordered to return to their reservations.

1876: The Lakota Sioux and U.S. Army begin a war.

1876: The Battle of the Little Bighorn takes place on June 25. Lieutenant Colonel Custer and all 210 of his men are killed.

1877: The U.S. government takes the remaining land in the Black Hills region.

1877: Sitting Bull leads his followers to Canada in search of food.

1879: The Little Bighorn battlefield is designated a national cemetery.

1881: Sitting Bull and his followers return to the United States. They surrender, and Sitting Bull is imprisoned.

1883: Sitting Bull moves to Standing Rock reservation.

1885: Sitting Bull tours with Buffalo Bill's Wild West show.

1889: The Ghost Dance religious movement begins.

1890: Sitting Bull is killed on December 15 as he is being arrested by Native American police.

1953: Sitting Bull's remains are moved to Mobridge, South Dakota, where a monument marks his grave.

1980: In *United States v. Sioux Nation of Indians*, the Supreme Court awards the Sioux $105 million for the Black Hills land taken from them in 1877. However, the Sioux reject the money and demand to have their original territory returned.

1991: The Custer Battlefield is formally renamed the Little Bighorn Battlefield.

1999: The first red granite grave markers are unveiled to honor Native American warriors who died in the battle.

GLOSSARY

CAUTIOUS Careful or taking special care to avoid problems ahead of time.

CAVALRY Troops mounted on horseback.

HOLY MAN A Native American tribe member who is an expert at medicines and sacred tribal rituals.

MEMORIAL Something that keeps alive the memory of a person or event.

MONUMENT A building, pillar, stone, or statue honoring a person or event.

OUTSPOKEN Direct and open in speech or expression.

RAID A sudden attack or invasion.

RESERVATION An area of public lands reserved for use by Native Americans.

SYMBOL Something real that stands for or suggests another thing that cannot in itself be pictured or shown.

TEPEE A cone-shaped tent, usually made of skins, used as a home.

TREATY An agreement or arrangement made between two or more states or rulers by negotiation.

WARLIKE To be fond of war.

FOR MORE INFORMATION

BOOKS

Collard, Sneed B. *Sitting Bull: "Tatanka Iyotake."* New York, NY: Marshall Cavendish Benchmark, 2010.

McDonnell, Julia. *Sitting Bull in His Own Words.* New York, NY: Gareth Stevens Publishing, 2015.

Reis, Ronald A. *Sitting Bull.* New York, NY: Chelsea House, 2010.

Spinner, Stephanie. *Who Was Sitting Bull?* New York, NY: Grosset & Dunlap, 2014.

Stanley, George Edward. *Sitting Bull: Great Sioux Hero.* New York, NY: Sterling, 2010.

WEBSITES

Because of the changing nature of Internet links, Rosen Publishing has developed an online list of websites related to the subject of this book. This site is updated regularly. Please use this link to access this list:

http://www.rosenlinks.com/BBB/Bull

INDEX